EVERYDAY
Thanksgiving

Other Soul Deep Scripture Journals
from *Sweet To The Soul Ministries*

31-Day Scripture Journals:

New Life

Love Is

Grace

God's Masterpiece

I Believe

Let Your Light Shine

7-Day Scripture Journals:

Together We're Better

Rest for the Weary Soul

All proceeds from the sale of Soul Deep devotionals, journals and other materials, go towards providing Soul Deep Bible study materials *free of charge* to women incarcerated in prison or living in a shelter.

At the heart of Sweet To The Soul Ministries is the desire to share God's Word with women. To Encourage the Study of God's Divinely Inspired Word.

EVERYDAY
Thanksgiving

A 31 - Day Soul Deep Scripture Journal

soul deep
SCRIPTURE JOURNAL

Everyday Thanksgiving :

A Soul Deep Scripture Journal

Copyright © 2016 by Sweet To The Soul Ministries
All rights reserved.

www.SweetToTheSoul.com

Illustrations: Copyright © 2016 Jana Kennedy-Spicer

Cover Design by: Jana Kennedy-Spicer
Interior Design by: Jana Kennedy-Spicer

ISBN-13: 978-1539602903

ISBN-10: 1539602907

CreateSpace Independent Publishing Platform, North Charleston, SC

Introduction

Just a few weeks ago, my husband and I were enjoying some time away in the mountains of New Mexico. The bright golden color of aspen trees with changing leaves combined with the cool crisp air was soul refreshing for this Texas girl. Although it was still hot at home, there in the mountains, my favorite season was in full display.

Autumn. Ahhhh.

Yes, my favorite season. But not for the weather, although the cooler temps are very welcome after 100° summer days. And not for the colors, even though there is nothing like the beauty of the fiery red and golden leaves fluttering in the breeze.

No autumn is my favorite time of year because as the season changes, it seems attitudes also change and a sense of "gathering" sets in as the holidays are just around the corner.

Thanksgiving and Christmas.

True thanksgiving, though, is so much more than a holiday or a by-product of changing seasons.

True thanksgiving is a heart condition displayed in our normal day to day life.

True thanksgiving is everyday thanksgiving.

When we say "thank you" to someone is it typically for something - something they've said that made us feel good or something they've done which we appreciate. This is a lovely and right expression. But this isn't the type of thanksgiving we are called to by God's Word.

Biblical thanksgiving is much deeper than a mere expression or note card.

> **"Give thanks in all circumstances,**
> **for this is the will of God in Christ Jesus for you."**
> 1 Thessalonians 5:18

Biblical thanksgiving is not based on our circumstances, it is in spite of our circumstances.

*"Giving thanks always and for everything to God the Father
in the name of our Lord Jesus Christ."*
Ephesians 5:20

Biblical thanksgiving is not an occasional feeling or spoken word, it is an always attitude.

These scriptures teach us that:

1. True thanksgiving is present in all of our circumstances—
    good or bad, easy or hard, beneficial or costly.

2. True thanksgiving is present in all of our days—
    short or long, calm or stressful. Celebratory or mournful.

3. *True thanksgiving is everyday thanksgiving.*

Soul Friends, I look forward to this 31-day journey through the Bible as we dive soul deep each day in to God's Word to learn how we can live a life of everyday thanksgiving.

Blessings,

How to Use This Scripture Journal

For awhile now, I've been praying the same prayer, every day. "Lord, create in me a desire for Your Word." It's short. It's simple. But it's soul deep. And it's a prayer, I feel, God finds joy in answering. So I've put together this Scripture Journal for me to use each day, and I would love to share it with you and invite you on this journey with me as we dive #souldeep into God's Word.

There are a couple of ways to use this Scripture Journal. But either way is at your own pace. If you've just got 10 minutes, go ahead and dive in; and if you've got more time, then let's get soul deep in the scriptures.

So, grab your Bible, a pen, some colored pencils or highlighters – and let's dive in!

Soul Deep Scripture

1. Read: today's scripture
2. Reflect: what does this scripture mean (use the verse mapping exercise)
3. Relate: how do I apply this scripture to my life
4. Pray: talk to God about today's scripture and topic
5. Remember: what is today's key take-a-way

Verse Mapping

1. Read the verse.
2. Write out your verse. (in this box, leave plenty of space around it, between the lines and between the words.)
3. Personalize it: replace words like "you", "we", "us", "them" with your name.
4. Mark, circle, underline, highlight words and phrases that stand out to you. Any words make you want to dig deeper? Look up and define any words that need clarification.
5. Read the verse in context: read the preceding and following verses or whole chapter. See how it ties in to the verses before and after it.
6. Read the verse in other translations: note which words or phrases help you understand or apply the verse.
7. Cross-reference the verse: find, list and read other verses which speak about the same topic.

soul deep
Scripture Journal

Daily Reading List

EVERYDAY
Thanksgiving

1. Read
2. Reflect
3. Relate
4. Pray
5. Remember

☐ 1   1 Thessalonians 2:13
☐ 2   Colossians 3:17
☐ 3   Philippians 1:3
☐ 4   Psalm 79:13
☐ 5   1 Chronicles 16:35
☐ 6   1 Timothy 2:1
☐ 7   Isaiah 51:3
☐ 8   Psalm 118:21
☐ 9   Romans 1:8
☐ 10   1 Thessalonians 3:9
☐ 11   Daniel 2:23
☐ 12   Philippians 4:6
☐ 13   Psalm 95:2
☐ 14   1 Chronicles 16:34
☐ 15   1 Timothy 1:12
☐ 16   Ephesians 5:4
☐ 17   Psalm 109:30
☐ 18   Revelation 11:17
☐ 19   1 Corinthians 15:57
☐ 20   Colossians 3:15
☐ 21   Luke 2:38
☐ 22   Psalm 75:1
☐ 23   1 Chronicles 23:30
☐ 24   2 Corinthians 9:11-12
☐ 25   Jeremiah 30:19
☐ 26   Psalm 142:7
☐ 27   Romans 6:17
☐ 28   1 Chronicles 29:13
☐ 29   2 Thessalonians 1:3
☐ 30   Luke 17:15-16
☐ 31   Psalm 28:7

SOUL DEEP SCRIPTURE

DATE:

READ "And we also thank God constantly for this, that when you received the word of God, which you heard from us, you accepted it not as the word of men but as what it really is, the word of God, which is at work in you believers." 1 Thessalonians 2:13

REFLECT

RELATE

pray

REMEMBER

VERSE MAPPING

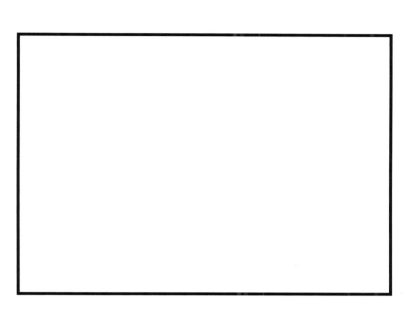

CROSS-REFERENCE

WORD STUDY

SOUL DEEP SCRIPTURE

DATE:

READ "And whatever you do, in word or deed, do everything in the name of the Lord Jesus, giving thanks to God the Father through him." Colossians 3:17

REFLECT

RELATE

pray

REMEMBER

VERSE MAPPING

CROSS-REFERENCE

WORD STUDY

READ

"I thank my God in all my remembrance of you," Philippians 1:3

REFLECT

RELATE

pray

REMEMBER

VERSE MAPPING

WORD STUDY

READ

"But we your people, the sheep of your pasture, will give thanks to you forever; from generation to generation we will recount your praise." Psalm 79:13

REFLECT

RELATE

PRAY

REMEMBER

VERSE MAPPING

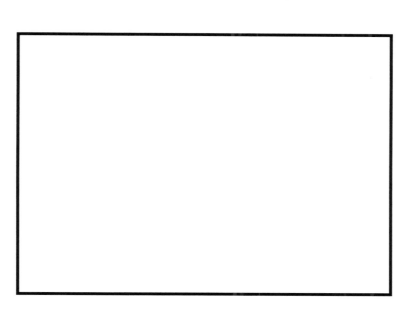

CROSS-REFERENCE

WORD STUDY

READ

"For great is the LORD, and greatly to be praised, and he is to be feared above all gods." 1 Chronicles 16:35

REFLECT

RELATE

pray

REMEMBER

Verse Mapping

Cross-Reference

Word Study

SOUL DEEP SCRIPTURE

DATE:

READ "First of all, then, I urge that supplications, prayers, intercessions, and thanksgivings be made for all people," 1 Timothy 2:1

REFLECT

RELATE

pray

REMEMBER

VERSE MAPPING

CROSS-REFERENCE

WORD STUDY

SOUL DEEP SCRIPTURE

DATE:

READ "For the LORD comforts Zion; he comforts all her waste places and makes her wilderness like Eden, her desert like the garden of the LORD; joy and gladness will be found in her, thanksgiving and the voice of song." Isaiah 51:3

REFLECT

RELATE

pray

REMEMBER

VERSE MAPPING

CROSS-REFERENCE

WORD STUDY

LET YOUR SOUL BE *Inspired*

We your people the sheep of Your pasture will Give thanks to you Forever from Generation to Generation we will recount your praise

PSALM 79:13

READ

"I thank you that you have answered me and have become my salvation."
Psalm 118:21

REFLECT

RELATE

pray

REMEMBER

VERSE MAPPING

CROSS-REFERENCE

WORD STUDY

SOUL DEEP SCRIPTURE

DATE:

READ "First, I thank my God through Jesus Christ for all of you, because your faith is proclaimed in all the world." Romans 1:8

REFLECT

RELATE

 pray

REMEMBER

VERSE MAPPING

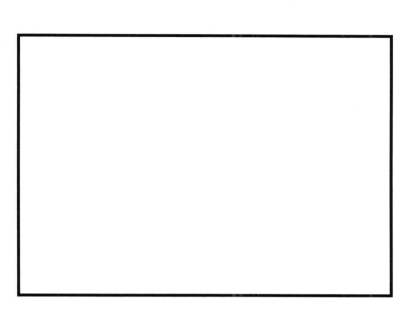

CROSS-REFERENCE

WORD STUDY

SOUL DEEP SCRIPTURE

DATE:

READ

"For what thanksgiving can we return to God for you, for all the joy that we feel for your sake before our God," 1 Thessalonians 3:9

REFLECT

RELATE

pray

REMEMBER

VERSE MAPPING

CROSS-REFERENCE

WORD STUDY

READ "To you, O God of my fathers, I give thanks and praise, for you have given me wisdom and might, and have now made known to me what we asked of you, for you have made known to us the king's matter."" Daniel 2:23

REFLECT

RELATE

PRAY

REMEMBER

Verse Mapping

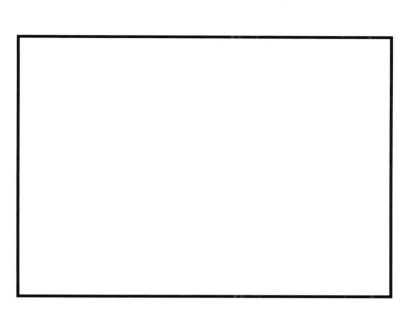

Cross-Reference

Word Study

READ

"do not be anxious about anything, but in everything by prayer and supplication with thanksgiving let your requests be made known to God." Philippians 4:6

REFLECT

RELATE

pray

REMEMBER

VERSE MAPPING

CROSS-REFERENCE

WORD STUDY

Soul Deep Scripture

DATE:

READ "Let us come into his presence with thanksgiving; let us make a joyful noise to him with songs of praise!" Psalm 95:2

REFLECT

RELATE

pray

REMEMBER

VERSE MAPPING

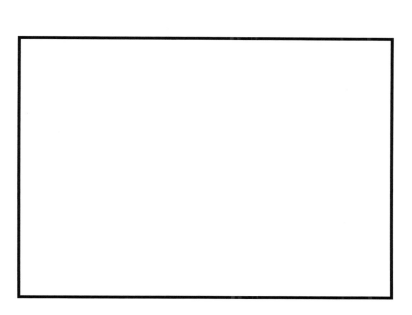

CROSS-REFERENCE

WORD STUDY

SOUL DEEP SCRIPTURE

DATE:

READ

"Oh give thanks to the LORD, for he is good; for his steadfast love endures forever!"
1 Chronicles 16:34

REFLECT

RELATE

REMEMBER

Verse Mapping

Cross-Reference

Word Study

LET YOUR SOUL BE *Inspired*

do not be
ANXIOUS
ABOUT anything BUT IN
EVERYthing
by PRAYER & SUPPLICATION with
Thanksgiving
let your REQUESTS
be made known to God
~ Philippians 4:6 ~

SOUL DEEP SCRIPTURE

DATE:

READ "I thank him who has given me strength, Christ Jesus our Lord, because he judged me faithful, appointing me to his service," 1 Timothy 1:12

REFLECT

RELATE

pray

REMEMBER

VERSE MAPPING

CROSS-REFERENCE

WORD STUDY

Soul Deep Scripture

DATE:

READ

"Let there be no filthiness nor foolish talk nor crude joking, which are out of place, but instead let there be thanksgiving." Ephesians 5:4

REFLECT

RELATE

pray

REMEMBER

Verse Mapping

Cross-Reference

Word Study

READ

"With my mouth I will give great thanks to the LORD; I will praise him in the midst of the throng." Psalm 109:30

REFLECT

RELATE

pray

REMEMBER

Verse Mapping

Cross-Reference

Word Study

DAY
18

Soul Deep Scripture

Date:

READ "We give thanks to you, Lord God Almighty, who is and who was, for you have taken your great power and begun to reign." Revelation 11:17

REFLECT

RELATE

pray

REMEMBER

VERSE MAPPING

CROSS-REFERENCE

WORD STUDY

Soul Deep Scripture Journal

SOUL DEEP SCRIPTURE

DATE:

READ "But thanks be to God, who gives us the victory through our Lord Jesus Christ."
1 Corinthians 15:57

REFLECT

RELATE

pray

REMEMBER

VERSE MAPPING

CROSS-REFERENCE

WORD STUDY

DAY 20

SOUL DEEP SCRIPTURE

DATE:

READ "And let the peace of Christ rule in your hearts, to which indeed you were called in one body. And be thankful." Colossians 3:15

REFLECT

RELATE

pray

REMEMBER

Verse Mapping

Cross-Reference

Word Study

READ

"And coming up at that very hour she began to give thanks to God and to speak of him to all who were waiting for the redemption of Jerusalem." Luke 2:38

REFLECT

RELATE

pray

REMEMBER

VERSE MAPPING

CROSS-REFERENCE

WORD STUDY

LET YOUR SOUL BE *Inspired*

and let the peace of Christ rule in Your Hearts to which indeed you were called IN ONE BODY and be.. Thankful

Colossians 3:15

SOUL DEEP SCRIPTURE

DATE:

READ

"We give thanks to you, O God; we give thanks, for your name is near. We recount your wondrous deeds." Psalm 75:1

REFLECT

RELATE

pray

REMEMBER

Verse Mapping

Cross-Reference

Word Study

Soul Deep Scripture

DATE:

READ

"And they were to stand every morning, thanking and praising the LORD, and like-wise at evening," 1 Chronicles 23:30

REFLECT

RELATE

pray

REMEMBER

VERSE MAPPING

CROSS-REFERENCE

WORD STUDY

SOUL DEEP SCRIPTURE

DATE:

READ

"You will be enriched in every way to be generous in every way, which through us will produce thanksgiving to God. For the ministry of this service is not only supplying the needs of the saints but is also overflowing in many thanksgivings to God. "
2 Corinthians 9:11-12

REFLECT

RELATE

pray

REMEMBER

VERSE MAPPING

CROSS-REFERENCE

WORD STUDY

SOUL DEEP SCRIPTURE

DATE:

READ "Out of them shall come songs of thanksgiving, and the voices of those who celebrate. I will multiply them, and they shall not be few; I will make them honored, and they shall not be small." Jeremiah 30:19

REFLECT

RELATE

pray

REMEMBER

VERSE MAPPING

CROSS-REFERENCE

WORD STUDY

DAY
26

SOUL DEEP SCRIPTURE

DATE:

READ "Bring me out of prison, that I may give thanks to your name! The righteous will surround me, for you will deal bountifully with me." Psalm 142:7

REFLECT

RELATE

pray

REMEMBER

VERSE MAPPING

CROSS-REFERENCE

WORD STUDY

DAY
27

SOUL DEEP SCRIPTURE

DATE:

READ "But thanks be to God, that you who were once slaves of sin have become obedient from the heart to the standard of teaching to which you were committed,"
Romans 6:17

REFLECT

RELATE

 pray

REMEMBER

VERSE MAPPING

CROSS-REFERENCE

WORD STUDY

READ

"And now we thank you, our God, and praise your glorious name." 1 Chronicles 29:13

REFLECT

RELATE

pray

REMEMBER

VERSE MAPPING

CROSS-REFERENCE

WORD STUDY

AND NOW WE thank you OUR God AND Praise YOUR Glorious NAME

FIRST CHRONICLES 29:13

SOUL DEEP SCRIPTURE

DATE:

READ "We ought always to give thanks to God for you, brothers, as is right, because your faith is growing abundantly, and the love of every one of you for one another is increasing." 2 Thessalonians 1:3

REFLECT

RELATE

pray

REMEMBER

Verse Mapping

Cross-Reference

Word Study

SOUL DEEP SCRIPTURE

DAY
30

DATE:

READ

"Then one of them, when he saw that he was healed, turned back, praising God with a loud voice; and he fell on his face at Jesus' feet, giving him thanks. Now he was a Samaritan." Luke 17:15-16

REFLECT

RELATE

REMEMBER

VERSE MAPPING

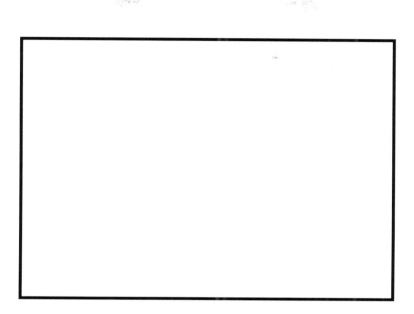

CROSS-REFERENCE

WORD STUDY

SOUL DEEP SCRIPTURE

DATE:

READ

"The LORD is my strength and my shield; in him my heart trusts, and I am helped; my heart exults, and with my song I give thanks to him." Psalm 28:7

REFLECT

RELATE

pray

REMEMBER

VERSE MAPPING

CROSS-REFERENCE

WORD STUDY

SCRIPTURE
Memory Cards

Scripture Memorization Tips

These scripture cards can be clipped to create individual double-sided scripture cards.

Once clipped, laminate for extra durability.

Punch a hole in the corner and place them on a ring to keep them handy.

Tack one up on the bulletin board or on the frig with a magnet and they will be close by as you go through your day.

Memorizing scripture may seem difficult, but it is vital to hiding God's Word in our heart. Here are some tips which may help you as you practice memorizing scripture:

1. Break the scripture into smaller sections or phrases.

2. Repeat the first phrase 3 times.

3. Repeat the next phrase 3 times.

4. Now repeat the first phrase together with the next phrase 3 times.

5. Continue this process until you have recited the entire scripture 3 times.

6. Don't forget to add the scripture reference!

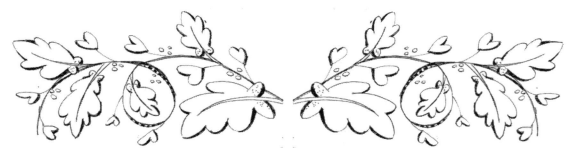

"And we also thank God constantly for this, that when you received the word of God, which you heard from us, you accepted it not as the word of men but as what it really is, the word of God, which is at work in you believers."
1 Thessalonians 2:13

"And whatever you do, in word or deed, do every-thing in the name of the Lord Jesus, giving thanks to God the Father through him."
Colossians 3:17

"I thank my God in all my remembrance of you,"
Philippians 1:3

"But we your people, the sheep of your pasture, will give thanks to you forever; from generation to generation we will recount your praise."
Psalm 79:13

"For great is the LORD, and greatly to be praised, and he is to be feared above all gods."
1 Chronicles 16:35

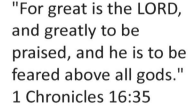

"First of all, then, I urge that supplications, prayers, inter-cessions, and thanksgivings be made for all people,"
1 Timothy 2:1

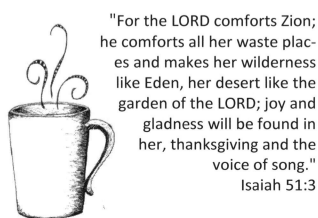

"For the LORD comforts Zion; he comforts all her waste plac-es and makes her wilderness like Eden, her desert like the garden of the LORD; joy and gladness will be found in her, thanksgiving and the voice of song."
Isaiah 51:3

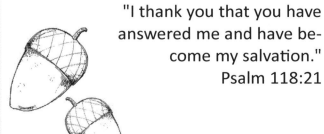

"I thank you that you have answered me and have be-come my salvation."
Psalm 118:21

"First, I thank my God through Jesus Christ for all of you, because your faith is proclaimed in all the world."
Romans 1:8

"For what thanksgiving can we return to God for you, for all the joy that we feel for your sake before our God,"
1 Thessalonians 3:9

"To you, O God of my fathers, I give thanks and praise, for you have given me wisdom and might, and have now made known to me what we asked of you, for you have made known to us the king's matter." Daniel 2:23

"do not be anxious about anything, but in everything by prayer and supplication with thanksgiving let your requests be made known to God."
Philippians 4:6

"Let us come into his presence with thanks-giving; let us make a joyful noise to him with songs of praise!"
Psalm 95:2

"Oh give thanks to the LORD, for he is good; for his steadfast love endures forever!"
1 Chronicles 16:34

"I thank him who has given me strength, Christ Jesus our Lord, because he judged me faithful, appointing me to his service,"
1 Timothy 1:12

"Let there be no filthiness nor foolish talk nor crude joking, which are out of place, but instead let there be thanksgiving."
Ephesians 5:4

"With my mouth I will give great thanks to the LORD; I will praise him in the midst of the throng."
Psalm 109:30

"We give thanks to you, Lord God Almighty, who is and who was, for you have taken your great power and begun to reign."
Revelation 11:17

"But thanks be to God, who gives us the victory through our Lord Jesus Christ."
1 Corinthians 15:57

"And let the peace of Christ rule in your hearts, to which indeed you were called in one body. And be thankful."
Colossians 3:15

"And coming up at that very hour she began to give thanks to God and to speak of him to all who were waiting for the redemption of Jerusalem."
Luke 2:38

"We give thanks to you, O God; we give thanks, for your name is near. We recount your wondrous deeds."
Psalm 75:1

"And they were to stand every morning, thanking and praising the LORD, and likewise at evening,"
1 Chronicles 23:30

"You will be enriched in every way to be generous in every way, which through us will produce thanksgiving to God. For the ministry of this service is not only supplying the needs of the saints but is also overflowing in many thanksgivings to God. "
2 Corinthians 9:11-12

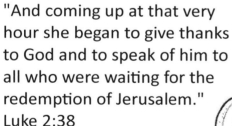

"Out of them shall come songs of thanksgiving, and the voices of those who celebrate. I will multiply them, and they shall not be few; I will make them honored, and they shall not be small."
Jeremiah 30:19

"Bring me out of prison, that I may give thanks to your name! The righteous will surround me, for you will deal bountifully with me."
Psalm 142:7

"But thanks be to God, that you who were once slaves of sin have become obedient from the heart to the standard of teaching to which you were committed,"
Romans 6:17

"And now we thank you, our God, and praise your glorious name."
1 Chronicles 29:13

"We ought always to give thanks to God for you, brothers, as is right, because your faith is growing abundantly, and the love of every one of you for one another is increasing."
2 Thessalonians 1:3

"Then one of them, when he saw that he was healed, turned back, praising God with a loud voice; and he fell on his face at Jesus' feet, giving him thanks. Now he was a Samaritan."
Luke 17:15-16

"The LORD is my strength and my shield; in him my heart trusts, and I am helped; my heart exults, and with my song I give thanks to him."
Psalm 28:7

EVERYDAY Thanksgiving

www.SweetToTheSoul.com

Soul Deep Scripture Journals

Dive in to God's Word with each of our 31-day Daily Scripture Reading plans. Designed to allow the user to spend time studying the Bible at their own pace. Use the Scripture Journals daily or at your own preferred schedule. Spend 10 minutes or 2 hours.

Let Your Light Shine

Finding New Life in Christ

You Are God's Masterpiece

31 Days of Grace

Soul Deep Scripture Journals

Visit our website to access our full line of Soul Deep Scripture Journals, Soul Deep Devotionals, Prayer Journals, and Bible Journaling materials.

www.SweetToTheSoul.com

Learning What Love Is

I Believe : What Do You Believe?

Also available are our **FREE** 7-Day **Soul Deep Mini-Series Scripture Journals.**

"Gracious words are as a honeycomb,

and healing to the bones."

Proverbs 16:24

Made in the USA
Monee, IL
03 November 2019